THE
CIRCULATORY
SYSTEM

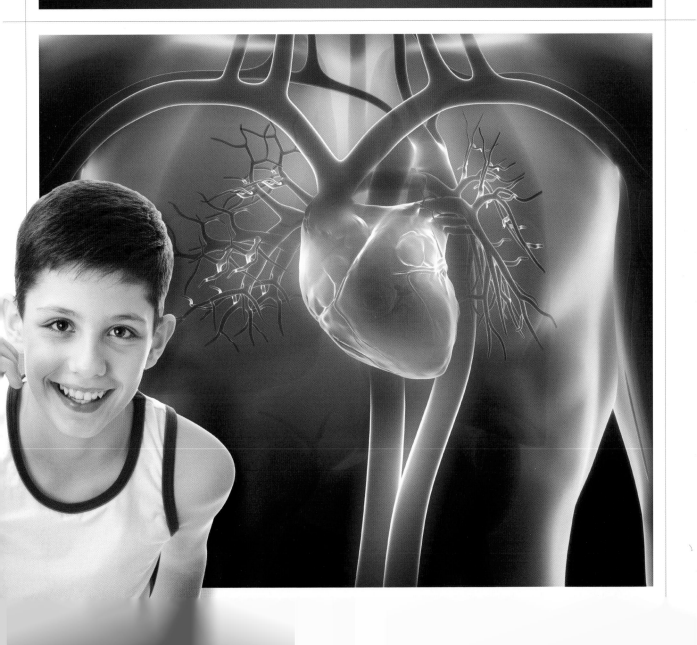

Published by The Child's World®
1980 Lookout Drive • Mankato, MN 56003-1705
800-599-READ • www.childsworld.com

Acknowledgments
The Child's World®: Mary Berendes, Publishing Director
Red Line Editorial: Editorial direction
The Design Lab: Design
Amnet: Production

Content Consultant: R. John Solaro, Ph.D., Distinguished University
Professor and Head, Department of Physiology and Biophysics,
University of Illinois Chicago

Photographs ©: CLIPAREA/Custom Media/Shutterstock Images,
cover (background), 1 (background); Sergiy N/Shutterstock
Images, cover (foreground), 1 (foreground); Denis Kuvaev/
Shutterstock Images, 4; BlueRingMedia/Shutterstock Images, 6;
Alexander Raths/Shutterstock Images, 9; iStockphoto, 11;
Purestock/Thinkstock, 12; Fuse/Thinkstock, 15; Digital Media
Pro/Shutterstock Images, 16; iStockphoto/Thinkstock, 19;
Wave Break Media/Shutterstock Images, 20

ISBN 9781626873346
LCCN 2014930671

Printed in the United States of America
Mankato, MN
July, 2014
PA02221

ABOUT THE AUTHOR

Susan H. Gray has a bachelor's and a master's degree in zoology. In her 25 years as an author, she has written many medical articles, grant proposals, and children's books. Ms. Gray and her husband, Michael, live in Cabot, Arkansas.

TABLE OF CONTENTS

CHAPTER 1

Nathan's Race

Nathan was ready for this race. He had practiced running all year. His whole school was cheering him on. The official fired his pistol. Nathan shot forward and raced down the track.

Running in a race takes a lot of energy.
Your circulatory system helps you keep moving.

Oxygen filled his lungs. The oxygen then moved into his blood. The oxygen-filled blood moved to his pounding heart. His heart pushed blood to the rest of his body. Nathan's muscle tissues took in the **nutrients** from the blood. This helped the tissues keep working.

As the tissues used the oxygen and nutrients, they made a gas called carbon dioxide. Blood moved the gas away from the tissues back to Nathan's heart. His heart sent the blood to his lungs again. The carbon dioxide then left Nathan's body. All of this happened in a few seconds.

Nathan could see the finish line. His legs were moving so fast and he was gasping for air. Nathan crossed the line barely ahead of his competition. His circulatory system had helped him win.

CHAPTER 2

What Is the Circulatory System?

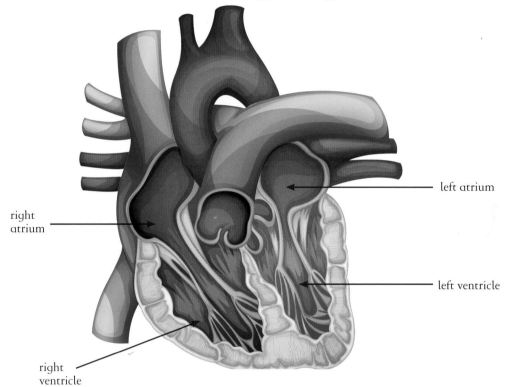

right atrium

left atrium

left ventricle

right ventricle

T he circulatory system moves blood to and from every part of the body. This system includes the blood, the heart, and all of the blood vessels. To circulate means to move around in a circle. Blood does not make

Despite their names, the left atrium and ventricle are found on the right side of the heart.

a circle as it flows through the body. But as blood moves, it keeps coming back through the heart.

The heart is the organ that pumps blood throughout the body. It has four sections, or chambers inside. Two chambers are in the top and two are in the bottom. Each top chamber is called an atrium. Each bottom chamber is called a ventricle. The heart has a right atrium and right ventricle. On the other side, it has a left atrium and left ventricle.

Each time the heart beats, it squeezes and forces blood out. Blood flows around the rest of the body through blood vessels. There are different kinds of blood vessels. They are the arteries, the capillaries, and the veins.

Blood flowing away from the heart moves through arteries. Arteries have muscular, **elastic** walls. The walls of the main arteries pulse, or throb, each time the heart beats. When you feel a pulse in your wrist or neck, you are feeling the throb of an artery. Arteries throb because of the blood surging through them.

Arteries farther from the heart are split up into smaller vessels. The vessels become so small they can be seen only with a microscope. These vessels are called capillaries.

After flowing through the capillaries, blood starts moving back to the heart. The tiny capillaries begin to come together. They join to form larger vessels. These vessels are called veins. They carry blood back to the heart. Vein walls are not as thick and muscular as those of arteries. And veins do not throb with each heartbeat. The inner walls of many veins have little flaps in them called valves. The valves come together to stop blood from moving backward. This keeps blood flowing toward the heart.

Blood moves through your arteries quickly. This is what you feel when you feel your pulse.

CHAPTER 3

What Is Blood?

Blood is a fluid that contains different materials. One of the materials is plasma. Plasma is made up mainly of water and is the color of straw. Plasma carries nutrients, red and white blood cells, and platelets throughout the body.

Most blood cells are red cells. Red blood cells look like a flattened donut. Red cells carry oxygen to the other cells in the body.

There are fewer white blood cells than red ones. But white blood cells have a very important job. They defend the body against germs that cause **infection**. White cells find germs that do not belong in the body. Sometimes white cells stick to the germ and destroy it.

> **DID YOU KNOW?**
> Deep inside certain bones, there is a red, spongy material called marrow. This is where the body makes blood cells.

Other times, white cells produce chemicals to attack the germ.

Blood also contains tiny platelets. They help the blood clot, or harden, when bleeding occurs. When a person gets a cut, platelets near the injury stick together. They form a little clump. The clump dries and becomes a scab.

CHAPTER 4

What Happens in the Heart?

The heart lies between the lungs. It is the pump that sends blood through the body. The heart is made of muscle tissue. It constantly squeezes and relaxes. This is the heart beating. When the heart

Blood is pumping through your circulatory system all day long.

beats, it pumps blood into the arteries. The blood returns to the heart through the veins.

When blood returns to the heart, it comes into the right atrium. The heart muscle squeezes, forcing blood through flaps. It moves down into the right ventricle. The heart muscle squeezes again, pushing blood into an artery. Blood flows through this artery and into the lungs.

The blood leaves the lungs and comes back to the heart. This time it comes into the left atrium. Then the heart beats again. Blood moves through another set of flaps and into the left ventricle. The heart muscle squeezes one more time. Blood then gushes into a large artery called the aorta. From there, the blood travels through blood vessels to every part of the body.

CHAPTER 5

Where Does Blood Go Next?

When blood leaves the left ventricle, it first goes through the aorta. Many arteries branch off from the aorta. Some of these arteries carry blood to the head. Some take blood to the arms and hands. Others carry blood to organs.

Arteries split into smaller vessels. Blood flows into these smaller vessels and into capillaries. The walls of capillaries are thin. Materials can actually move through these walls.

Capillaries are so small that blood cells barely fit. But very important things happen here.

Red cells let go of their oxygen. Other tissues in the area pick it up. All of the body's tissues need oxygen to work correctly. For example, muscles cannot move without oxygen. Hair and fingernails cannot grow without it. Eyes cannot see unless they get enough oxygen, and ears cannot hear without enough oxygen. These body parts get oxygen from red blood cells passing through the capillaries.

Red cells bring oxygen to all parts of the body.
Without oxygen, many body parts would not work.

Blood also brings nutrients to the tissues. Nutrients include sugars, fats, and minerals. Some nutrients give tissues their energy. Others help tissues to build

Your muscles need nutrients for energy.
The muscles get nutrients from your blood.

and grow. Nutrients move through the capillary walls. Nearby tissues take them and use them.

As the body's tissues work, they produce carbon dioxide. It is a waste material. Tissues need to get rid of it. Carbon dioxide moves into the capillaries and into the blood. Other waste materials from the tissues also move in. The blood then carries it all away.

A lot happens as blood slowly moves through the capillaries. Oxygen moves out to the tissues. Nutrients move out as well. Carbon dioxide and other wastes move into the blood. Then blood moves from the capillaries into the veins. And the veins carry blood back to the heart.

DID YOU KNOW?
Smaller animals tend to have faster heartbeats than larger animals. In flight, a hummingbird's heart beats more than 1,000 times per minute. A resting elephant's heart beats about 25 to 30 times per minute.

CHAPTER 6

What Happens in the Lungs?

When blood gets back to the heart, it contains carbon dioxide. Blood goes to the lungs for two important reasons. It gets rid of the carbon dioxide. And it picks up more oxygen.

The lungs are full of millions of tiny air **sacs.** Capillaries surround each of the sacs. These capillaries are like the ones in the rest of the body. They are so tiny that blood cells move through in single file. The capillary walls are thin, and gases can move through easily.

Each time you **inhale**, the air sacs fill up. Blood in the capillaries moves slowly past the sacs.

DID YOU KNOW?
At one time, people believed a person's heart produced thoughts and ideas. Now we know the brain does our thinking for us!

Carbon dioxide moves out of the blood and into the air sacs. Oxygen moves from the air sacs and into the blood. Then you **exhale**. Carbon dioxide goes out with the breath. And oxygen-filled blood continues on to the heart.

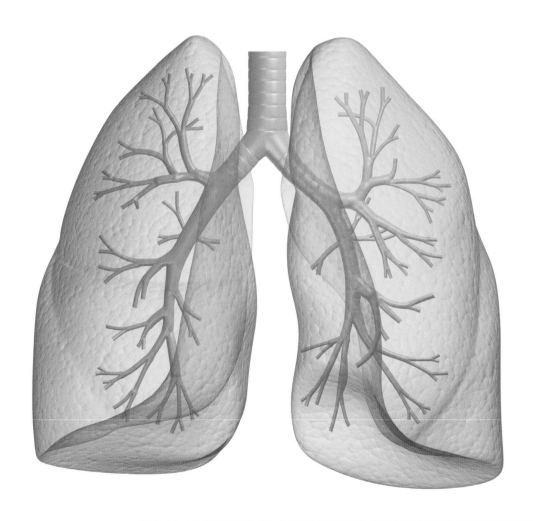

Oxygen fills your lungs and moves into the blood.
This blood then moves to your heart.

In an average day, a person inhales around 20,000 times. The heart beats more than 100,000 times. Billions of blood cells move through the capillaries. Gases come and go. In some people, the circulatory system does not work properly. Often this is because they have heart problems.

Some children are born with a hole in the wall between the right and left chambers. Each time the heart beats, blood from one side enters the other side. Blood from the left side could wash into the right side instead of going out to the rest of the body. Then the right side has to pump this extra blood to the lungs. Over time, this hard work could make the heart wear out. Small holes sometimes close up on their own. Surgery often takes care of the larger holes.

Adults sometimes have heart diseases, too. The best way to avoid any heart problems is to eat healthy foods and exercise. This helps your circulatory system do its amazing job.

Eating healthy and staying active will keep your circulatory system healthy, too.

GLOSSARY

elastic (i-LASS-tik) Something that is elastic is stretchy. Arteries have elastic walls.

exhale (eks-HAYL) To exhale means to breathe out. When you exhale, carbon dioxide leaves the body.

infection (in-FEK-shuhn) An infection is an illness that is caused by a germ or virus that has entered the body. White blood cells defend against infection.

inhale (in-HAYL) To inhale means to breathe in. When you inhale, your lungs fill up.

nutrients (NOO-tree-uhnts) Nutrients are the things found in foods that are needed for life and health. Plasma carries nutrients.

sacs (SAKS) Sacs are parts that are shaped like a little bag or pocket. The lungs are filled with millions of sacs.

LEARN MORE

BOOKS

Gardner, Jane P. *Take a Closer Look at Your Lungs.* Mankato, MN: The Child's World, 2014.

Manolis, Kay. *The Circulatory System.* Minneapolis: Bellwether Media, 2009.

Slike, Janet. *Take a Closer Look at Your Heart.* Mankato, MN: The Child's World, 2014.

WEB SITES

Visit our Web site for links about the circulatory system:
childsworld.com/links

Note to Parents, Teachers, and Librarians: We routinely verify our Web links to make sure they are safe and active sites. So encourage your readers to check them out!

INDEX